Guest Book

Copyright © Tabitha Leonard
All Rights Reserved.
No part of this publication can be used or reproduced in any manner whatsoever without written permission except in the case of brief quotations embodied in critical articles and reviews.
First Edition: 2021

In Celebration of

_____

_____

Date

_____

Venue

_____

_____

_____

Guests

Name   ## Message

Name   Message

Guests

Name   ## Message

Guests

Name

Message

Guests

Name   Message

Name   *Message*

Guests

Name   *Message*

Name *Message*

Guests

Name   ### Message

Name Message

Guests

Name   Message

Name   *Message*

Guests

Name   ### Message

Guests

Name

Message

Guests

Name

Message

Guests

Name

Message

Guests

Name

Message

Name   *Message*

Guests

Name   ### Message

Guests

Name

Message

Guests

Name

Message

Guests

Name

Message

Guests

Name　　　　　　　　　　　　　　　Message

Name

Message

Guests

Name

Message

Name   *Message*

Guests

Name   Message

Name

Message

Guests

Name   Message

Guests

Name

Message

Guests

Name ## Message

Name   *Message*

Guests

Name   Message

Name   Message

Guests

Name

Message

Name

Message

Guests

Name   ## Message

_____   _____
                                                      _____
                                                      _____
_____   _____
                                                      _____
                                                      _____
_____   _____
                                                      _____
                                                      _____
_____   _____
                                                      _____
                                                      _____

Name

Message

_____

_____

_____

_____

_____

_____

_____

_____

_____

_____

_____

_____

_____

_____

_____

_____

_____

_____

Guests

Name

Message

Guests

Name *Message*

Guests

Name   Message

Guests

Name

Message

Guests

Name   Message

Name

Message

Guests

Name   Message

Guests

Name

Message

Guests

Name   *Message*

Guests

Name   ## Message

Guests

Name   Message

Guests

Name   Message

Guests

Name   Message

Guests

Name　　　　　　　　　　　　　　　　Message

Guests

Name   Message

Guests

Name

Message

Guests

Name   Message

Name   Message

Guests

Name　　　　　　　　　　　　　Message

Guests

Name   Message

Name   *Message*

Name   *Message*

Guests

Name   Message

Guests

Name   ### Message

Guests

Name   ### Message

Guests

Name

Message

Guests

Name　　　　　　　　　　　　　　　　Message

Guests

Name

Message

Guests

Name   Message

Name   *Message*

Guests

Name   ## Message

Name   *Message*

Guests

Name   Message

Guests

Name

Message

Guests

Name

Message

Guests

Name   ## Message

Guests

Name

Message

Guests

Name

Message

Guests

Name   Message

Guests

Name

Message

Guests

Name *Message*

Guests

Name

Message

_____   _____
                                    _____
                                    _____
_____   _____
                                    _____
                                    _____
_____   _____
                                    _____
                                    _____
_____   _____
                                    _____
                                    _____

Guests

Name   ### Message

Guests

Name   *Message*

Guests

Name

Message

Name   Message

_____   _____

_____   _____

_____   _____

_____   _____

_____   _____

                                                                  _____

                                                                  _____

                                                                  _____

                                                                  _____

                                                                  _____

Guests

Name *Message*

Guests

Name

Message

Guests

Name   Message

Name Message

Guests

Name   Message

Guests

Name   Message

Guests

Name　　　　　　　　　　　　　　　Message

Guests

Name   Message

Guests

Name   ### Message

Guests

Name

Message

Guests

Name   *Message*

Name Message

Guests

Name

Message

Guests

Name

Message

Notes

Notes

Notes

Notes

Notes

Notes

Notes

Notes

Notes

Notes

Notes

Notes

Notes

Notes

Notes

Notes

Notes

Printed in Dunstable, United Kingdom